EX LIBRIS

For Joseph, David and Emily
J.W.

First published 1989 by
Walker Books Ltd, 87 Vauxhall Walk
London SE11 5HJ

Text © 1989 Jenny Koralek
Illustrations © 1989 Juan Wijngaard

First Printed 1989
Printed by South China Printing Co., Hong Kong

British Library Cataloguing in Publication Data
Koralek, Jenny
The Hanukkah.
1. Judaism, Hanukkah
I. Title   II. Wijngaard, Juan
296.4'35

ISBN 0-7445-1260-3

HANUKKAH

The Festival of Lights

Written by Jenny Koralek
Illustrated by Juan Wijngaard

WALKER BOOKS
London

Long, long ago a wicked king called Antiochus marched into the city of Jerusalem with many soldiers. At his cruel command the soldiers charged into the streets, set fire to the houses and killed hundreds of Jewish men, women and children.

Then the soldiers went into the Temple and stole out of it all the precious holy things. Worst of all they stole the great, seven-branched candlestick, called the menorah, which stood before the altar. And its flames went out. Such a thing had never happened before. They were God's dancing flames, kept alight with a special oil, kept in a special pot.

The king went back to his own country, but his soldiers stayed behind and brought great suffering and misery to the Jews. The invaders brought food and drink into the Temple. They shouted and laughed in the Temple. They played noisy games in the Temple. The Temple was no longer a place of peace and quiet where Jews could say their prayers.

Jews throughout the land were very frightened and very sad. All except one old man, Mattathias, who lived in a village below the hills of Jerusalem. He was very angry. He rose up and said, "All the weeping and the wailing in the world will not give us back our city and our Temple. We will have to fight to get them back. It will take a long time, because we are few and they are many. But in the end we will win and the Temple will be holy again."

Mattathias went into the mountain wilderness with his five sons, John, Simon, Judah the Maccabee, Eleazar and Jonathan. They hid in deep caves reached by paths known only to the people of the land. Other brave men soon joined them. They set about fighting the enemy with whatever weapons they could make or find. They always attacked suddenly, at unexpected times of day and night, then vanished swiftly, silently, among the rocks and boulders.

Then Mattathias fell ill. He knew he was dying, so he called his sons and said, "Together you must carry on the fight, but make Judah the Maccabee your leader. He has always been the strongest since you were children. And now on all sides I hear him called The Hammer. I believe God will bless his deeds. Keep your courage, my sons, and remember you are brothers."

Judah the Maccabee took his father's hand in his. "We will never stop fighting," he promised, "until once again the candles of the menorah are burning in the Temple."

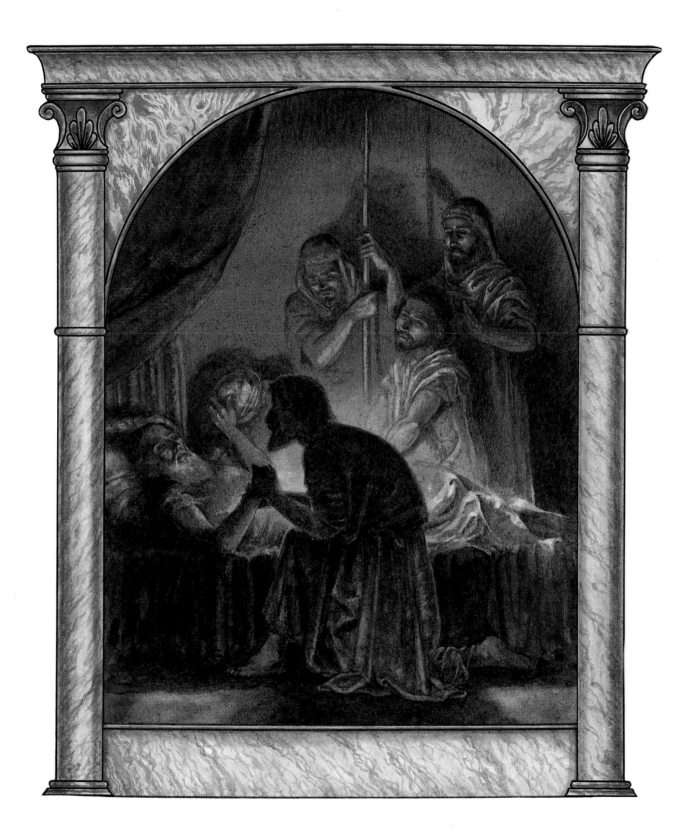

After the death of Mattathias the enemy grew even bolder. Thousands of soldiers took part in every battle. Some rode on horseback and some on elephants. But Judah the Maccabee and his men were not afraid of the huge, strange animals. They were not afraid of anything. For two long years they fought like lions up and down the land. And then, one starless night, they besieged Jerusalem.

Judah the Maccabee camped outside
Jerusalem all through the winter. The day
came when there was very little food left to
eat in the city, and very little water to drink
and only a little oil for cooking, or for
lighting candles. This was the moment he
had been waiting for. He stormed the gates.
He scaled the walls and chased the
enemy out.

21

The Jews were free again. They sang. They danced. They waved branches of palm trees. They played joyful music on harps and cymbals. And Judah the Maccabee smiled. "Come," he said, "let us all work together to clean the Temple and make it beautiful once more."

They cleaned the dark and dirty Temple from top to bottom. They put back the menorah, but, when they came to light it, they found only enough clean and holy oil to last one day. And Judah the Maccabee said, "Please God, give us time! Let the oil last till we have found some more! We have fought so long and so hard to be here again in the Temple. Please do not let the flames go out!"

God heard the prayer. The flames did not go out. For eight days they burned steadily and more and more brightly by the day. Then all the people in the land of the Jews came flocking into the Temple. They were filled with wonder to see the flames dancing in the winter darkness. And Judah the Maccabee said, "We must never forget these eight special days. From now on, every year at this time, we and our children and our children's children and so on down the ages will remember them with a joyful festival of lights."

To this very day, in the dark midwinter, many Jewish families keep that promise made by Judah the Maccabee. They take down a special candlestick and polish it and set it on a table, or in the window. For eight nights, as the first stars come out, they light one candle until all of them are burning brightly. They look into the flames and give thanks for that great miracle in the Temple of Jerusalem long, long ago.